G000155488

Rightness vs. Righteousness

By
Pastor Creflo A. Dollar Jr.

If you would like more information about this ministry, or are interested in becoming a partner, please write:
WORLD CHANGERS MINISTRIES
Post Office Box 490124
College Park, Georgia 30349

Editorial and Creative services provided by:
Vision Communications
169 E. 32nd
Edmond, OK 73013
(405) 348-7995

Cover design by:
Virgil Lynn Design
405-348-7965

Unless otherwise indicated, all Scripture quotations are from the KING JAMES VERSION.

AMP – Amplified Version
NIV – New International Version

Rightness vs. Righteousness
ISBN: 0-9634781-5-x

*This book is dedicated to
Bishop Kenneth & Sister Jean Fuller.
I thank God for you both.*

Table of Contents

Chapter 1
When Rightness is Wrong

"I know my rights!" It's a familiar cry in our society today. It seems as if everyone is consumed with making sure nobody violates or infringes on their rights.

Now don't get me wrong. I'm not against you exercising your rights. I thank God we live in a country in which we are guaranteed certain freedoms by our constitution.

But what if you encounter a situation in which standing up for your rights means stepping out of the will of God?

I believe we are moving into an historic time in which believers are going to be faced with such decisions in ever increasing numbers. Decisions that demand that you choose between "rightness" and "righteousness."

The choices you make in such situations are going to determine in large part how successful you are in the coming months and years.

In the following pages you'll see in God's Word how to recognize a "rightness vs. righteousness" situation and how to condition your flesh to respond correctly.

You'll also see how doing so brings God onto the scene in your behalf and puts you in a position to come out victoriously.

First, let's take a close look at the differences between rightness and righteousness.

Two Types of Righteousness
For they being ignorant of God's righteousness, and going about to establish their own righteousness, have not submitted themselves unto the righteousness of God. (Romans 10:3)

This verse clearly establishes that there are two kinds of righteousness. There is God's righteousness and there is man's righteousness or "rightness".

Rightness refers to the state of being right or correct. Have you ever known someone who always had to be right? Someone who just couldn't stand it unless you and everyone else knew that they were right all along? That's rightness.

God's righteousness, on the other hand, refers to up-rightness and virtue. It means, "in accordance with the dictates of God" and "free from guilt."

Righteousness forms the basis of your "rights" or "benefits" with God. When you have God's righteousness, you have the right to forgiveness of sin, the right to healing, the right to the presence and empowerment of the Holy Spirit, the right to success and the right to security.

You did not earn these rights. They are granted to you because of the love and mercy of God.

Yet few Christians are enjoying the benefits of those rights. Why? According to the passage of scripture above, because of "ignorance"! "For they being ignorant of God's righteousness, and going about to establish their own righteousness..."

Don't get the wrong idea. Ignorant does not mean "stupid." It simply means not knowing. Hosea 4:6 says "My people are destroyed for a lack of knowledge."

When you are ignorant of the nature of God's right-eousness, you don't know about the things to which you have a right. The result is that you endeavor to establish your own righteousness or rightness.

For example, many new Christians don't really know how to pray from a confident position in the righteous-ness of God. So they pray the way they've heard other religious people pray:

"Dear kind, heavenly Father. Once more we, your humble, good-for-nothing, lowly dog servants beseech you. We know we don't deserve anything, Lord...etc., etc.."

When we pray all that false humility garbage instead of standing in our position as sons and covenant partners of the Most High God, we're establishing our own standard of righteousness in prayer.

You can do the same thing in regard to giving. If, instead of bringing the whole tithe (10%) into the storehouse as God commands, you just give a little bit here and there when you feel like it, you're establishing your own rights in giving.

These are things new or immature believers do out of ignorance. Then, when they get into the Word and find out what it says about these matters, they are faced with the difficult task of breaking with their old religious traditions.

That break must take place, however. Traditions make the Word of God of no effect (Matthew 15:6).

Right or Righteous

Let me present a hypothetical situation. Suppose you get into a disagreement with someone over a business transaction. Suppose the other person cheated you out of some money.

Then suppose the Spirit of God tells you not to worry about it but rather let God take care of it. At that point you're faced with a decision. Do you do whatever is necessary to prove that you are right? After all you've been cheated! Or do you stand in the righteousness of God and trust him to move on your behalf?

The first course is to pursue rightness. The second course is to choose righteousness.

When you pursue rightness rather than righteousness you are concerned with being correct at any cost. Correct in the eyes of man, that is.

Righteousness, on the other hand, is concerned only with what God thinks. No opinion of man matters.

The two differ in others ways as well. Rightness is usually self-centered. It says, "I've got to look good before man in order to feel good about myself." When you have that attitude, you'll fight to your last breath to prove that you're right and the other person is wrong.

Rightness seeks self-gratification and approval from God through good works. In contrast, righteousness recognizes that you are accepted based on what Jesus has done through His blood and the cross.

The bottom line is, righteousness seeks to please God rather than self.

How does righteousness please God? By faith! Romans 3:22 tells us that righteousness is "by faith." And Hebrews 11:6 tells us that without faith it is impossible to please God.

Backed Up By Righteousness
Seek ye first the kingdom of God, and his righteousness and all these things shall be added unto you. (Matthew 6:33)

When you are bent on proving your "rightness" to other people, you leave God out of the picture. You're on your own. At that point you're easy prey for anything the devil wants to throw at you.

But when you seek God's righteousness first and foremost, God is committed to back you up every step of the way.

The first approach puts you in bondage to other people. The second places you in the liberating service of a loving God.

"But Pastor Dollar! You don't know what that person is saying about me! What about my reputation?"

Look. If you'll take care of your character, God will take care of your reputation. Just stay in the righteousness of God and operate in the fruit of the Spirit. When all is said and done, God will back you up and your reputation will be stronger and better than ever.

I'm not implying that reputation isn't important. It's vital that we, as people who name the Name of Jesus Christ abstain from the very appearance of evil.

I'm simply saying you don't have to run around de-fending yourself when people accuse you falsely or tell lies about you.

Take care of your character and God will look after your reputation. Psalm 9:3,4 guarantees it.

When mine enemies are turned back, they shall fall and perish at thy presence. For thou hast main-tained my right and my cause; thou satest in the throne judging right.

We all have enemies. Just don't get your eyes on them. Keep your focus on the one sitting on the throne. That vi-sion will fill you with confidence in knowing that Almighty God is taking up your cause.

That means you don't have to get in the flesh and do something that will probably make things worse.

Trust is the Key
But let all those that put their trust in thee rejoice: let them ever shout for joy, because thou defendest them: let them also that love thy name be joyful in thee. (Psalm 5:11)

The key to resting in the knowledge that God is your righteous back up, is trust.

When you are verbally attacked or treated unfairly, it is impossible to resist the natural urge defend yourself without a deep abiding trust in God.

Trust says, "I will not take up my own cause because God is my Defender. I will stand on the Word knowing that ultimately God will cause things to come out my way."

You can afford to be confident when you have the best attorney in the universe representing you. God is a lawyer who has never lost a case. Trust Him.

Whose Approval Are You After?
Study and be eager and do your utmost to present yourself to God approved (tested by trial), a work-

man who has no cause to be ashamed, correctly analyzing and accurately dividing–rightly handling and skillfully teaching-the Word of Truth. (II Timothy 2:15 AMP)

To avoid falling into the trap of "rightness" over "righteousness" you must orient your life toward the goal of God-approval rather than man-approval. As this verse indicates, that approval usually comes after you've been "tested by trial."

Many Christians claim to be committed to God and to His will, yet their commitment evaporates in the heat of trial.

Don't talk about your commitment one minute and present yourself to others for their approval the next. Present yourself to God for approval and prove your commitment by standing up under testing.

One of the keys to passing the test is found in the very next verse.

But avoid all empty (vain, useless, idle) talk, for it will lead people into more and more ungodliness. (II Timothy 2:16 AMP)

That's a pretty clear order. Avoid useless, idle talk because it leads people into ungodliness. The word "ungodliness" as it is used in this verse could also be translated "sedition" or "rebellion".

This type of thing happens very subtly. Someone makes a comment like, "I don't see why the pastor always has to talk about money."

What, on the surface, is a seemingly innocent observation is actually the beginning of sedition. That kind of idle talk leads to rebellion and eventually to failure.

Jesus, Our Example

When you are being lied about, cheated or treated unfairly, it's pretty easy to start thinking that you're the first person to ever suffer so unjustly. At those times it is a good idea to open your Bible to the second chapter of I Peter:

For this is thankworthy, if a man for conscience toward God endure grief, suffering wrongfully. For what glory is it, if, when ye be buffeted for your faults, ye shall take it patiently? but if, when ye do well, and suffer for it, ye take it patiently, this is acceptable with God. For even hereunto were ye called: because Christ also suffered for us, leaving us an example, that ye should follow his steps: Who did no sin, neither was guile found in his mouth: Who, when he was reviled, reviled not again; when he suffered, he threatened not; but committed himself to him that judgeth righteously: (I Peter 2:19-23)

Jesus is the ultimate example in dealing with undeserved persecution. He never defended himself. Why? Because He knew that if He would stay in faith and stay out of the way, God would be His Defender.

Over and over again, Jesus' enemies challenged his authority and attacked his motives. Yet He never allowed Himself to get into a defensive mode.

At the cross Jesus could have summoned legions of angels to come to his rescue. Instead He silently suffered the pain and humiliation of crucifixion.

Compared to that, our petty hurt feelings shrink into insignificance.

Chapter 2
The Covenant of Peace

We've seen how important it is to stay in the righteousness of God and not get off into your own "rightness."

To do that, there is one key ingredient that must be a part of your life. That ingredient is peace.

You must have peace in order to stay in God's righteousness and you must have God's righteousness to reap the results of peace.

The kind of peace I'm talking about involves a sense of security in the midst of turmoil. Rest in the middle of the storm.

It is a little like the feeling of security that comes with knowing that all your insurance premiums are paid up and you are fully covered. When a "fender bender" comes along you don't panic or lose your composure. You have peace because you know you're backed up by insurance.

Jesus has given you an insurance policy. It's the most comprehensive coverage you could ever imagine. And Jesus has paid all the premiums in full.

That policy is known as "the covenant of peace" and it is found in Isaiah chapter 54, verses 7-17.

Let's take a look at this marvelous insurance policy one benefit at a time.

For a small moment have I forsaken thee; but with great mercies will I gather thee. In a little wrath I hid my face from thee for a moment; but with everlasting kindness will I have mercy on thee, saith the LORD thy Redeemer. (v.7,8)

God's desire is to gather you with "great mercies" and to show you His "everlasting kindness."

When these verses talk about God's "wrath" and His hiding His face, it refers to God's pouring out the punishment for sin on Jesus on the cross.

There Jesus cried, "My God, why hast thou forsaken me." Because of what Jesus endured on the cross, God is free to have mercy on us and show us kindness.

For this is as the waters of Noah unto me: for as I have sworn that the waters of Noah should no more go over the earth; so have I sworn that I would not be wroth with thee, nor rebuke thee. (v.9)

Just as God promised Noah to never again destroy the earth by water, so He has promised to not be angry with those who appropriate Jesus' death on the cross to their lives.

For the mountains shall depart, and the hills be removed; but my kindness shall not depart from thee, neither shall <u>the covenant of my peace</u> be removed, saith the LORD that hath mercy on thee. (v.10)

All these promises and those that follow are part of this "covenant of peace."

A covenant is a solemn oath or contract between two parties. In this wonderful agreement, God graciously vows to be your ever-present back up.

He says, "Step back and relax little covenant partner. Let your big covenant partner come in and take care of you. You don't ever, ever have to worry about anything."

O thou afflicted, tossed with tempest, and not comforted, behold, I will lay thy stones with fair colours, and lay thy foundations with sapphires. And I will make thy windows of agates, and thy gates of carbuncles, and all thy borders of pleasant stones. (v.11,12)

Storms are a part of life. There's no getting around it. Just because you're a Christian doesn't mean you're never going to have any trouble.

Your covenant of peace, however, guarantees that in the midst of those storms you'll not only be anchored and established-you'll be crowned with jewels as well.

And all thy children shall be taught of the LORD; and great shall be the peace of thy children. (v.13)

The covenant of peace covers not only you but extends to your children as well. Your whole family is covered by this insurance policy.

If you have children who seem to be straying from the ways of the Lord, pull out your covenant of peace and show the devil your insurance policy.

Say, "Take your hands off my children, mister. This says that they all shall be taught of the Lord and great shall be their peace."

In righteousness shalt thou be established: thou shalt be far from oppression; for thou shalt not fear: and from terror; for it shall not come near thee. Behold, they shall surely gather together, but not by me: whosoever shall gather together against thee shall fall for thy sake. (v.14,15)

You will be established in what? "Righteousness." God's righteousness will establish you in such a way that fear, terror and oppression have no right to come near you.

When enemies accuse you falsely and try to destroy you, you can rest in your covenant of peace. You don't have to prove your "rightness." God's righteousness will establish you and cause those who gather together against you to fall.

Behold, I have created the smith that bloweth the coals in the fire, and that bringeth forth an instrument for his work; and I have created the waster to destroy. No weapon that is formed against thee shall prosper; and every tongue that shall rise against thee in judgment thou shalt condemn. (V.16,17)

This is a powerful covenant! No weapon...No weapon formed against you can prosper or succeed.

Consider all the weapons aimed at your family right now. There are weapons of violence, weapons of disease, weapons of lack, strife and fear. Yet when you stand on your rights granted through your covenant of peace, none of them can succeed against you.

Notice God didn't say that no weapons would be formed. Just that those that are formed could not prosper.

This covenant even extends to deal with those who would dare to speak against you unjustly. "Every tongue that shall rise against you in judgement you shall condemn."

When someone speaks evil of you, you don't have to go running around trying to defend yourself. Just rest in your covenant of peace.

This is the heritage of the servants of the LORD, and their righteousness is of me, saith the LORD. (v.17)

All the benefits just mentioned are the rightful heritage or inheritance of the servants of the Lord. Why? Because "their righteousness is of me, says the Lord."

Submitting to and operating in God's righteousness rather than your own rightness makes these promises a reality in your life.

Chapter 3
Jesus, Prince of Peace

And there arose a great storm of wind, and the waves beat into the ship, so that it was now full. And he was in the hinder part of the ship, asleep on a pillow: and they awake him, and say unto him, Master, carest thou not that we perish? And he arose, and rebuked the wind, and said unto the sea, Peace, be still. And the wind ceased, and there was a great calm. And he said unto them, Why are ye so fearful? how is it that ye have no faith? (Mark 4:37-40)

This passage of scripture paints a vivid picture of the two types of responses you can have when confronted by one of the inevitable storms of life.

On one hand you have the reaction of the disciples. Panic-stricken, fearful, full of doubt, convinced that they are all about to die.

On the other, you have Jesus. So completely calm and at rest that He's sleeping, even though the boat is tossing violently and filling up with water.

Why was Jesus at peace in the midst of an apparent crisis? He understood his covenant with God.

You see, in verse 35 Jesus had said, "Let's get in the boat and cross over to the other side of the lake." In effect, the word had been given. The Son of God had spoken. The disciples had a clear command from the Word made flesh. "Cross over to the other side."

Had they possesed any understanding of the covenant of peace they would have relaxed saying, "If Jesus said we're going over to the other side then we will surely make it."

That's why Jesus marvelled at their unbelief. "How is it that ye have no faith?"

Many Christians make the same mistake the disciples did. A storm of life comes along and they start to panic.

A bad report from the doctor, a late notice from a bill collector or a rumor of layoffs at work. And suddenly we're crying, "Oh Jesus! Don't you care that we're perishing?!"

Instead of wallowing in all that fear and unbelief you need to do what Jesus demonstrated-yell "PEACE!" "BE STILL!"

No storm of life will ever harm you if will hold on to your covenant of peace. Stand on the Word of God. Declare, "By His stripes I am healed!" "My God supplies all my needs according to His riches in glory by Christ Jesus!" "No weapon formed against me shall prosper!"

And remember, the covenant of peace is not yours because of your righteousness. It belongs to you as you abide in God's righteousness.

As a born-again child of God you not only have the righteousness of God, you are the righteousness of God.

For he hath made him to be sin for us, who knew no sin; that we might be made the righteousness of God in him. (II Corinthians 5:21)

You see, there's no need to try to prove yourself right. Stay in the righteousness of God and all the security and rest that comes through the covenant of peace will be yours.

Confession

In the name of Jesus, I walk after God's righteousness and not my own righteousness. I will not perish because of ignorance or a lack of knowledge. Rather, I will study to show myself approved a workman who does not need to be ashamed. I rightly divide the Word of Truth.

My covenant partner, the Most High God, is my Defender. I will rejoice and be exceedingly glad because He has never lost a case.

I thank you Father for your covenant of peace. Because of it, I have security in the midst of the storm. Fear and frustration have no place in my life. Worry has no place in my thinking. I walk in the peace of God and in the comfort of the Holy Ghost.

I now receive the covenant of peace in Jesus' name. Amen.

Tape Series by Pastor Creflo A. Dollar Jr.

The Blessings of Obedience

The Blood Covenant

By Faith in His Presence

Confidence: The Missing Substance of Faith

The Creative Power of Words

Deliverance from Lasciviousness

Destroying the Root of Debt

The Divine Order of Faith:
From the Problem to the Answer

Enemies of Faith

Faith, Foolishness or Presumption

Family and Marriage Convention '92

Forces of the Reborn Spirit

Foundation Principles of the Christian Life

Freedom from Fear

The Fruit of the Spirit

God Wants You Healed – Healing Convention 1992

God's Blessing of Prosperity

God's Plan for the Christian Family

God's Purpose for the Anointing

The Grand Finale – The Book of Revelation

Hearing and Obeying God's Voice

Hindrances to Faith

How to…By God's Word

How to Defeat the Devil

How to Experience a Deeper Life in Prayer

Intercessory Prayer

The Law of Harvest

Lifestyle of Faith

Man's Heart: The Workshop of God

The Mercies of God

Obtaining the Wealth of the Wicked

Overcoming Faith

The Power of the Anointed Word

The Power and Integrity of God's Word

Prayer: The Rock of Success

The Price to Pay to Hear from God

Pride or Humility: You Choose

The Principles of Praise

The Rejuvenation of Faith

The Rejuvenation of Prayer

The Seven Steps of Answered Prayers

Spiritual Warfare

Temptations

Things that will close the Windows of Heaven

True Worship and Praise

Understanding God's Principles of Holiness

Understanding God's Way to Financial Prosperity – Finance Convention '92

Understanding the Seasons of Sowing and Reaping

Unmasking the Devil and His Deceptions

The Weapons of Prayer

Unforgiveness: A Hindrance to Faith

How to Believe with the Heart (Part I)

How to Believe with the Heart (Part II)

Revival